F·R·I·E·N·D·S

FRIENDS

F·R·I·E·N·D·S

B☐XTREE

First published in the US by Andrews and McMeel, a Universal Press Syndicate Company, 4900 Main Street, Kansas City, Missouri 64112

First published in the UK in 1996 by Boxtree Limited, Broadwall House, 21 Broadwall, London SE1 9PL by special arrangement with Warner Bros. Worldwide Publishing

ISBN: 0 7522 2232 5

10 9 8 7 6 5 4 3

Printed and bound in Hong Kong

A CIP catalogue entry for this book is available from the British Library

Contents

MEET
THE
FRIENDS

monica

Beautiful and bright, but a tad uptight, she keeps a tidy apartment and a very messy romantic life.

Job: Chef at an uptown restaurant

Telling quote: "Don't look now, but behind you there is a guy who has the potential to break our hearts and plunge us into a pit of depression."

ross

Monica's older brother, he's smart,
sensitive, and a proud new daddy. The
only hitch is that the baby's mother
left him for a woman.

Job: Paleontologist (dinosaur
bone guy)

Telling quote: "It's just . . . well,
you know the whole getting-on-
with-your-life thing. Do I have to?"

rachel

After walking out on her fiance and her well-to-do family, she's making the jump from debutante princess to coffeehouse waitress.

Job: Hopelessly inept waitress

Telling quote: "Okay, I know this is going to sound really stupid—but I feel that if I can do this, if I can actually do my own laundry, there isn't anything I can't do."

chandler

With a lightning-quick wit and a smart-ass attitude, he's valiantly resisting the pull of the corporate (and adult) world.

Job: An undefined middle-management accounting-type position in which he has no interest whatsoever. His responsibilities include analyzing the WEENUS (Weekly Estimated Net Usage Statistics).

Telling quote: "Things sure have changed here on Walton's Mountain."

A bit dense, but earnest and likable,
he's a handsome womanizer and
struggling (really struggling) actor.

Job: Infrequent stage actor and
one-time butt-double for Al Pacino.

Telling quote: "When I'm with a woman,
I need to know that I'm going out with
more people than she is."

phoebe

Supremely flaky but very sweet,
she writes new songs and coins new
words with equal proficiency.

Job: Part-time masseuse who also plays
her guitar and sings in the subway.

Telling quote: "Debbie, my best friend
in junior high, got struck by lightning
on a miniature golf course. And I
always get this really strong Debbie vibe
whenever I use one of those little
yellow pencils."

HOOKING UP

Friends on Dating

Monica on discovering that her new boyfriend is in high school:
Oh God, I'm like those women you see with shiny guys named Chad. I'm Joan Collins.

●●●

Chandler: I think, for us, kissing is pretty much an opening act. I mean, it's like the comedian you have to sit through before Pink Floyd comes up.
Rachel: Yeah, well, word of advice—bring back the comedian. Otherwise, next time you're going to find yourself sitting at home listening to that album alone.

Phoebe encouraging Chandler to approach a beautiful woman:
You know how you always see, like, some really beautiful women with these really nothing guys? You could be one of those guys.

• • •

Rachel: I can't believe he hasn't kissed you yet. God, by my sixth date with Paolo, he'd already named both my breasts.

• • •

Phoebe: I broke up with Roger. . . . I mean, he's a good person. And he can be really sweet. And in some ways I think he's so right for me. It's just . . . I hate that guy.

Joey discussing Ross's romantic history:
Man, can you believe he's only had sex
with one woman?
Chandler: I think that's great. You know,
it's sweet. It's romantic . . .
Joey: Really?
Chandler: Are you kidding?
The guy's a freak.

• • •

Ross: Wasn't this supposed to be a fling.
Shouldn't it be . . . flung by now?

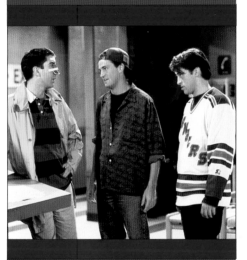

Joey advising Chandler against appearing too eager after a great first date:
Let her dangle.

...

Phoebe: Oh, come on! Just do it! Call her! Stop being so . . . testosteroney.
Chandler: Which, by the way, is the <u>real</u> San Francisco treat.

...

Monica: Joey, stop hitting on her. It's her wedding day.
Joey: What? Like there's some rule or something?

The Secret Language of Dating

Monica: Loosely translated, "We should do this again" means "You will never see me naked."

Rachel: Since when?

Joey: Since always. It's like dating language. You know, like . . . "It's not you" means "It is you."

Chandler: Or "You're such a nice guy" means "I'm gonna be dating leather-wearing alcoholics and complaining about them to you."

Phoebe: Or, you know, um . . . "I think we should see other people" means "Ha, ha . . . I already am."

Ross: I figured after work, I'd pick up a bottle of wine, go over there, and try to . . . woo her.

Chandler: Hey, you know what you should do? Take her back to the 1890s when that phrase was last used.

• • •

Chandler to Ross: What are you still doing here? She just broke up with the guy. It's time for you to swoop in.

• • •

Joey to Ross: It's never gonna happen between you and Rachel. Because, you waited too long to make your move, and now you're in the "Friend Zone."

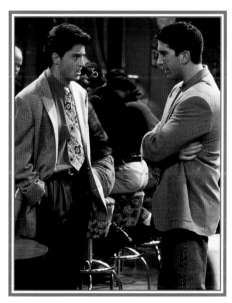

Monica to her male friends:
I can't believe my parents are actually pressuring me to find one of you people.

• • •

Phoebe on the art of breaking up:
You can do this. It's just like pulling off a Band-Aid™. You do it really fast and then the wound is exposed.

• • •

Monica: Is it me? Is it like I have a beacon that only dogs and men with severe emotional problems can hear?

DYSFUNCTIONALLY YOURS

Friends on Family

Rachel: Why can't parents just stay parents? Why do they have to become people?

• • •

Monica: Chandler, you're an only child, right? You didn't have any of this.
Chandler: Well, no. Although I did have an imaginary friend who my parents actually preferred.

• • •

Phoebe, jealous of her twin:
It's mostly dumb sister stuff. She was the first one to start walking, even though I did it the same day. But to my parents, by then it was, yeah, like, "Right, what else is new?"

Ross, after completing his childbirth classes:
You could plunk me down in the middle of any woman's uterus, no compass, and I could find my way out of there (snaps fingers) like that.

• • •

Ross: I had a dream last night where I was playing football with my kid.
Chandler: Oh, yeah? That's nice.
Ross: No. No. With him. I'm on this field, and they hike me the baby.

Joey to Ross: You broke the code . . .
You don't kiss your friend's mom.
Sisters are okay, maybe a hot lookin'
aunt, but not a mom, never a mom.

• • •

Chandler: If I turn into my parents,
I'll either be an alcoholic blond chasing
twenty-two-year-old boys, or I'll wind up
like my mom.

• • •

Rachel on seeing Ross's baby for the
first time:
I can't believe one of us actually has
one of these.
Chandler: I know. I still *am* one of these.

MY SO-CALLED CAREER

Friends
on Working

Chandler: Well, you know, Pheebs, I don't know if being a secretary is your kind of thing, because it involves a lot of being normal for a large portion of the day.

• • •

Rachel on viewing her first paycheck: Who's FICA? Why is he getting my money?

• • •

Monica to Rachel: Welcome to the real world. It sucks. You're gonna love it.

Chandler: You can always spot someone who's never seen one of Joey's plays before. Notice: No fear. No sense of impending doom.

•••

Phoebe to Joey after he admits to participating in a fertility study to earn extra cash:
Wow, you're gonna make money hand over fist.

•••

Rachel: Well, you ladies are not the only ones living the dream. I get to go pour coffee for people I don't know.
Don't wait up.

Rachel: I've sort of been maintaining my amateur status so I can waitress in the Olympics.

• • •

Chandler: All right, kids, I've got to get to work. If I don't input those numbers . . . it doesn't make much of a difference.

• • •

Chandler: Hey, you guys all know what you want to do. You know, you have goals. You have dreams. I don't have a dream.

Ross: Ah, the lesser known "I Don't Have A Dream" speech.

HANGING OUT

A Few Good Friends

Monica: Come on. Let's get some coffee.
Chandler: Oh, okay. 'Cause we never do that.

· · ·

Ross, on Marcel the monkey's sexual awakening:
One day Marcel's a little thing. And then, before you know it, he's this little thing I can't get off my leg.

· · ·

Joey: Hey, I don't need violence to enjoy a movie. So long as there's a little nudity.

· · ·

Ross: I've got to go to China.
Joey: The country?
Ross: No. The big pile of dishes in my mom's breakfront.

Monica: We thought since Phoebe was staying over, we'd make it kind of a slumber party thing. We got trashy magazines, we got cookie dough, we got Twister . . .

Phoebe: Oooh! And I brought Operation— but I lost the tweezers, so we can't operate. But we can prep the guy.

•••

Chandler: I believe this piece of furniture was fine until your little breakfast adventure with Angela Delvecchio.

Joey: You knew about that?

Chandler: Well, let's just say the impressions you made in the butter left little to the imagination.

PHOEBEISMS

Exploring the Outer Limits of Language

*New York City has no power.
All the milk is turning sour.
But to me that's not so scary.
'Cause I stay away from dairy.
LA LA LA LA LA LA LA . . .

*You're like Mr. Caring Boss. Mr. I'm
One of You Boss. I want to Be Your
Buddy Boss Man Bing.

*If you're up to your fifteenth date,
you're in a very relationshippy place,
you know.

*It's my friends. They have a "liking"
 problem with you. In that, um, they don't.

*What's the matter? Why so scrunchy?

*You're like all chaotic and twirly.
 And not in the good way.

*Where are you going, Mr. Suity-Man.

*I'm going to miss you, you scientist guy.

*And for a shrink, he's not too "shrinky."

DOIN' THE BING THING

Chandler's Comebacks

Chandler illustrating his unenviable
situation:
Okay. Rock. Hard place. Me.

Chandler, as Ross enters the room with
Marcel on his shoulder:
Hey, that monkey's got a Ross on his
ass.

Joey: Go to China. Eat Chinese food.
Chandler: Of course, there they just
call it "food."

Chandler: You know that thing when you and I talk to each other about things?

Joey: Yeah.

Chandler: Let's not do that anymore.

...

Ross: I can't even get Marcel to stop eating the bathmat. How am I going to raise a kid?

Chandler: You know, Ross, some scientists are now saying that monkeys and babies are actually different.

Joey: All right. You're a monkey. You're loose in the city. Where do you go?

Chandler: Okay, it's his first time out, so he's probably going to want to do some of the touristy things. I'll go to "Cats," you go to The Russian Tea Room.

...

Ross: All right. All right, we're all adults here. There's only one way to resolve this: Since you saw her boobies, I think you're going to have to show her your pee-pee.

Chandler: You know, I don't see that happening.

Rachel: Come on. He's right. Tit for tat.

Chandler: Well, I am not showing you my tat.

Chandler in response to Monica's news that "Paul the Wine Guy" asked her out: Oh, this is a dear diary moment.

• • •

Chandler: So? How'd it go?
Joey: It was amazing. You know how you always think you're great in bed?
Chandler: The fact that you even ask that question shows how little you know me.

Chandler on learning that Rachel is babysitting Ross's monkey:
I can't remember the last time I got a girl to take care of my monkey.

• • •

Chandler: How about "Joey Pepponi"?
Joey: No, still too ethnic. My agent thinks I should have a name that's more neutral.
Chandler: "Joey Switzerland"?